Francis Frith's
AROUND SALISBURY

PHOTOGRAPHIC MEMORIES

Francis Frith's
AROUND SALISBURY

◆

Les Moores

FRITH
BOOK Co

First published in the United Kingdom in 1999 by
Frith Book Company Ltd

Paperback Edition 2000
ISBN 1-85937-239-2

Hardback Reprinted in 2000
ISBN 1-85937-091-8

British Library Cataloguing in Publication Data

Around Salisbury
Les Moores

Frith Book Company Ltd
Frith's Barn, Teffont,
Salisbury, Wiltshire SP3 5QP
Tel: +44 (0) 1722 716 376
Email: info@frithbook.co.uk
www.frithbook.co.uk

Printed and bound in Great Britain

AS WITH ANY HISTORICAL DATABASE THE FRITH ARCHIVE IS CONSTANTLY BEING CORRECTED AND IMPROVED
AND THE PUBLISHERS WOULD WELCOME INFORMATION ON OMISSIONS OR INACCURACIES

CONTENTS

FRANCIS FRITH: *Victorian Pioneer*

FRANCIS FRITH, Victorian founder of the world-famous photographic archive, was a complex and multitudinous man. A devout Quaker and a highly successful Victorian businessman, he was both philosophic by nature and pioneering in outlook.

By 1855 Francis Frith had already established a wholesale grocery business in Liverpool, and sold it for the astonishing sum of £200,000, which is the equivalent today of over £15,000,000. Now a multi-millionaire, he was able to indulge his passion for travel. As a child he had pored over travel books written by early explorers, and his fancy and imagination had been stirred by family holidays to the sublime mountain regions of Wales and Scotland. 'What a land of spirit-stirring and enriching scenes and places!' he had written. He was to return to these scenes of grandeur in later years to 'recapture the thousands of vivid and tender memories', but with a different purpose. Now in his thirties, and captivated by the new science of photography, Frith set out on a series of pioneering journeys to the Nile regions that occupied him from 1856 until 1860.

INTRIGUE AND ADVENTURE

He took with him on his travels a specially-designed wicker carriage that acted as both dark-room and sleeping chamber. These far-flung journeys were packed with intrigue and adventure. In his life story, written when he was sixty-three, Frith tells of being held captive by bandits, and of fighting 'an awful midnight battle to the very point of surrender with a deadly pack of hungry, wild dogs'. Sporting flowing Arab costume, Frith arrived at Akaba by camel seventy years before Lawrence, where he encountered 'desert princes and rival sheikhs, blazing with jewel-hilted swords'.

During these extraordinary adventures he was assiduously exploring the desert regions bordering the Nile and patiently recording the antiquities and peoples with his camera. He was the first photographer to venture beyond the sixth cataract. Africa was still the mysterious 'Dark Continent', and Stanley and Livingstone's historic meeting was a decade into the future. The conditions for picture taking confound belief. He laboured for hours in his wicker dark-room in the sweltering heat of the desert, while the volatile chemicals fizzed dangerously in their trays. Often he was forced to work in remote tombs and caves where conditions were cooler. Back in London he exhibited his photographs and was 'rapturously cheered' by members of the Royal Society. His reputation as a photographer was made overnight. An eminent modern historian has likened their impact on the population of the time to that on our own generation of the first photographs taken on the surface of the moon.

VENTURE OF A LIFE-TIME

Characteristically, Frith quickly spotted the opportunity to create a new business as a specialist publisher of photographs. He lived in an era of immense and sometimes violent change. For the poor in the early part of Victoria's reign work was a drudge and the hours long, and people had precious little free time to enjoy themselves.

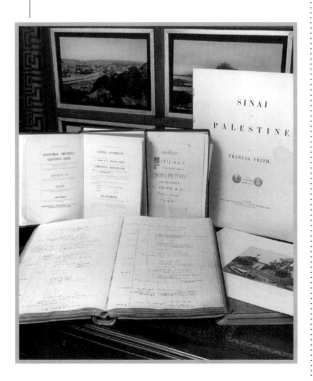

Most had no transport other than a cart or gig at their disposal, and had not travelled far beyond the boundaries of their own town or village. However, by the 1870s, the railways had threaded their way across the country, and Bank Holidays and half-day Saturdays had been made obligatory by Act of Parliament. All of a sudden the ordinary working man and his family were able to enjoy days out and see a little more of the world.

With characteristic business acumen, Francis Frith foresaw that these new tourists would enjoy having souvenirs to commemorate their days out. In 1860 he married Mary Ann Rosling and set out with the intention of photographing every city, town and village in Britain. For the next thirty years he travelled the country by train and by pony and trap, producing fine photographs of seaside resorts and beauty spots that were keenly bought by millions of Victorians. These prints were painstakingly pasted into family albums and pored over during the dark nights of winter, rekindling precious memories of summer excursions.

THE RISE OF FRITH & CO

Frith's studio was soon supplying retail shops all over the country. To meet the demand he gathered about him a small team of photographers, and published the work of independent artist-photographers of the calibre of Roger Fenton and Francis Bedford. In order to gain some understanding of the scale of Frith's business one only has to look at the catalogue issued by Frith & Co in 1886: it runs to some 670

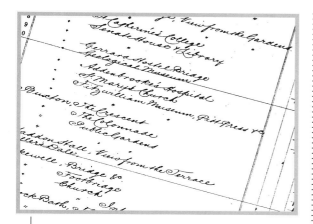

court card, but there was little room for illustration. In 1899, a year after Frith's death, a new card measuring 5.5 x 3.5 inches became the standard format, but it was not until 1902 that the divided back came into being, with address and message on one face and a full-size illustration on the other. *Frith & Co* were in the vanguard of postcard development, and Frith's sons Eustace and Cyril continued their father's monumental task, expanding the number of views offered to the public and recording more and more places in Britain, as the coasts and countryside were opened up to mass travel.

Francis Frith died in 1898 at his villa in Cannes, his great project still growing. The archive he created continued in business for another seventy years. By 1970 it contained over a third of a million pictures of 7,000 cities, towns and villages. The massive photographic record Frith has left to us stands as a living monument to a special and very remarkable man.

pages, listing not only many thousands of views of the British Isles but also many photographs of most European countries, and China, Japan, the USA and Canada – note the sample page shown above from the hand-written *Frith & Co* ledgers detailing pictures taken. By 1890 Frith had created the greatest specialist photographic publishing company in the world, with over 2,000 outlets – more than the combined number that Boots and WH Smith have today! The picture on the right shows the *Frith & Co* display board at Ingleton in the Yorkshire Dales. Beautifully constructed with mahogany frame and gilt inserts, it could display up to a dozen local scenes.

POSTCARD BONANZA

The ever-popular holiday postcard we know today took many years to develop. In 1870 the Post Office issued the first plain cards, with a pre-printed stamp on one face. In 1894 they allowed other publishers' cards to be sent through the mail with an attached adhesive halfpenny stamp. Demand grew rapidly, and in 1895 a new size of postcard was permitted called the

Frith's Archive: *A Unique Legacy*

FRANCIS FRITH'S legacy to us today is of immense significance and value, for the magnificent archive of evocative photographs he created provides a unique record of change in 7,000 cities, towns and villages throughout Britain over a century and more. Frith and his fellow studio photographers revisited locations many times down the years to update their views, compiling for us an enthralling and colourful pageant of British life and character.

We tend to think of Frith's sepia views of Britain as nostalgic, for most of us use them to conjure up memories of places in our own lives with which we have family associations. It often makes us forget that to Francis Frith they were records of daily life as it was actually being lived in the cities, towns and villages of his day. The Victorian age was one of great and often bewildering change for ordinary people, and though the pictures evoke an impression of slower times, life was as busy and hectic as it is today.

We are fortunate that Frith was a photographer of the people, dedicated to recording the minutiae of everyday life. For it is this sheer wealth of visual data, the painstaking chronicle of changes in dress, transport, street layouts, buildings, housing, engineering and landscape that captivates us so much today. His remarkable images offer us a powerful link with the past and with the lives of our ancestors.

TODAY'S TECHNOLOGY

Computers have now made it possible for Frith's many thousands of images to be accessed almost instantly. In the Frith archive today, each photograph is carefully 'digitised' then stored on a CD Rom. Frith archivists can locate a single photograph amongst thousands within seconds. Views can be catalogued and sorted under a variety of categories of place and content to the immediate benefit of researchers. Inexpensive reference prints can be created for them at the touch of a mouse button, and a wide range of books and other printed materials assembled and published for a wider, more general readership - in the next twelve months over a hundred Frith local history titles will be published! The

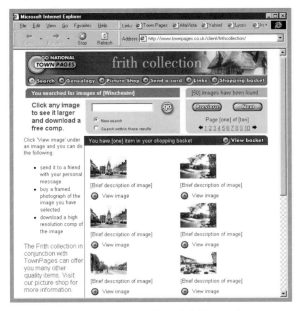

See Frith at www. francisfrith.co.uk

day-to-day workings of the archive are very different from how they were in Francis Frith's time: imagine the herculean task of sorting through eleven tons of glass negatives as Frith had to do to locate a particular sequence of pictures! Yet the archive still prides itself on maintaining the same high standards of excellence laid down by Francis Frith, including the painstaking cataloguing and indexing of every view.

It is curious to reflect on how the internet now allows researchers in America and elsewhere greater instant access to the archive than Frith himself ever enjoyed. Many thousands of individual views can be called up on screen within seconds on one of the Frith internet sites, enabling people living continents away to revisit the streets of their ancestral home town, or view places in Britain where they have enjoyed holidays. Many overseas researchers welcome the chance to view special theme selections, such as transport, sports, costume and ancient monuments.

We are certain that Francis Frith would have heartily approved of these modern developments, for he himself was always working at the very limits of Victorian photographic technology.

THE VALUE OF THE ARCHIVE TODAY

Because of the benefits brought by the computer, Frith's images are increasingly studied by social historians, by researchers into genealogy and ancestry, by architects, town planners, and by teachers and schoolchildren involved in local history projects. In addition, the archive offers every one of us a unique opportunity to examine the places where we and our families have lived and worked down the years. Immensely successful in Frith's own era, the archive is now, a century and more on, entering a new phase of popularity.

THE PAST IN TUNE WITH THE FUTURE

Historians consider the Francis Frith Collection to be of prime national importance. It is the only archive of its kind remaining in private ownership and has been valued at a million pounds. However, this figure is now rapidly increasing as digital technology enables more and more people around the world to enjoy its benefits.

Francis Frith's archive is now housed in an historic timber barn in the beautiful village of Teffont in Wiltshire. Its founder would not recognize the archive office as it is today. In place of the many thousands of dusty boxes containing glass plate negatives and an all-pervading odour of photographic chemicals, there are now ranks of computer screens. He would be amazed to watch his images travelling round the world at unimaginable speeds through network and internet lines.

The archive's future is both bright and exciting. Francis Frith, with his unshakeable belief in making photographs available to the greatest number of people, would undoubtedly approve of what is being done today with his lifetime's work. His photographs, depicting our shared past, are now bringing pleasure and enlightenment to millions around the world a century and more after his death.

SALISBURY – *An Introduction*

JUST A MILE OR TWO NORTH of present day Salisbury is the site of Old Sarum. It started life as an iron-age hill fort, became the small Roman town of Sorviodunum and eventually the Saxon village of Old Sarum, set on top of its hill overlooking the marshy land at the confluence of the Avon and several other rivers draining Salisbury Plain. In spite of being close to several ancient track ways and Roman roads, it never thrived as a settlement: it was safe but unpleasant - the opposite of nearby Wilton, with which it gradually began to suffer by comparison. Nevertheless, the Normans decided in 1075 to build a cathedral at Old Sarum. By 1218 the Bishop had decided they had made a terrible mistake - there was not even a decent water supply on the top of their hill - and a new site was chosen for his cathedral a mile or two to the south, on marshy ground where the Avon is joined by the Nadder.

Thus Salisbury, or New Sarum, was born - the only city in Wiltshire, and the only 'new' medieval city built round a new cathedral in the country. Three quarters of a millennium later, it is the one city which has somehow managed to preserve its medieval ambience almost intact. It could be said that this survival has been more through luck than judgement - sometimes even by default - but whatever the reasons, an astonishing amount of the infra-structure and the fabric of the original city still remains.

The cathedral itself (architecturally unique and crowned by the tallest spire in the county) was begun in 1220 and substantially completed within forty years. By 1260 the street pattern of the new town had been laid out and largely built up, based on a large market place. The plan was that of a staggered grid pattern enclosing rectangular 'chequers', with the roads doubling up as canals to provide both water and drainage for the flat, marshy site. Protected on two sides by the river, the city was defended on the other two sides by ramparts: Salisbury quickly became a great ecclesiastical and commercial centre, and by 1330 it was the tenth most important town in England.

Since Victorian times the city has grown at an increasing pace - but nothing like as fast as most other towns based on industrial development. Salisbury has always been an ecclesiastical, agricultural and administrative centre based on the traditional rural industries of farming, textiles (wool and leather), food and drink. More recently, it has been service industry which has dominated local employment; even though modern transport links have made the city an important communications centre, there has never been much heavy industrial development. Although it has never been a great garrison town, the city has, for the last century and a half, had close links with the military, being the largest town near

virtually every view is instantly recognisable today. In Salisbury, not only the Cathedral and the Close have survived, but so too has the medieval street pattern, together with its buildings (the churches, shops and houses) and the spaces between the buildings. City centre redevelopment is always a relative phenomenon, and in Salisbury change has usually been small in scale and spread out in time so that its psychological impact is somehow filtered and easier to assimilate. It is like a con-

the important training area on Salisbury Plain to the north.

In some ways, Salisbury has even become a bit of a backwater, and this has turned out to be a mixed blessing. It is not a particularly prosperous city (and Salisbury is no longer a rich diocese), and it is plagued by contemporary ills such as traffic congestion; but because so much of the original city remains, it possesses an amazing architectural, historic and photogenic legacy for the benefit of the present generation of residents, tourists and students.

The photographs in this collection go back in time almost a century and a half, yet

tinuum, and the camera of Francis Frith is the ideal medium for recording the thousands of almost imperceptible changes that are taken for granted and go almost unnoticed, yet add up over a period of time - in this case an unbroken 750 years - to progress.

The Cathedral was the reason for Salisbury's very existence, and it has dominated the city and the south Wiltshire landscape since it was built. Quite simply, it is a stunning architectural tour-de-force, built almost entirely in the same style (Early English Gothic) in one continuous operation over a relatively short time: this gives it a unique symmetry and unity of design making it even more impressive. After the spire; the cloisters and the chapter house were completed in the 14th century; building work stopped, although parts have been added and removed since, and several bouts of 'restoration' have taken place, what we have today is essentially what was there more than six centuries ago.

The whole building was constructed in Chilmark Stone, quarried from a ravine ten miles west of Salisbury near the village of Chilmark and almost identical to Portland Stone, which only came into fashion several centuries later when Sir Christopher Wren started using it on his public buildings in London.

The Close, which provides the physical setting for the cathedral, has survived as well. Built originally to house the clergy, it was begun at the same time as the Cathedral itself, and some of the buildings are of the same age. The Close (the largest in the country) was enclosed by a wall built in the 14th century along three sides (the River Avon ran along the other one) to protect the clergy from the population of the city outside. This was no idle threat: in medieval times the church was often unpopular, and the Bishop of Salisbury in particular suffered at the hands of the local mob. Even today, by tradition, the gates in the Close wall are locked shut each night.

The architectural heritage that survives in the Close is almost as precious as the cathedral itself: many of the century's finest architects - Sir Christopher Wren, James Wyatt, Augustus Pugin and Sir Giles Gilbert Scott for example - have worked here, although we do not know for sure who actually 'designed' the Cathedral. Because of the pattern of land ownership and use in the Close, even less seems to have altered here over the years. But insidious change is everywhere, and nowhere escapes completely: more and more vehicular and pedestrian traffic is attracted to the Close each year, and this can be traced in the photographs.

There are many old cathedral cities in England, but none has kept its medieval city centre intact to the same extent as Salisbury. Traffic in the 21st century is funnelling through the same streets that accommodated

the livestock and the carts of the 13th. This is impossible in any other city, and logically and politically it should not be possible even in Salisbury. However, apart from one ring road round the north of the city, and several large car parks, Salisbury has been spared the wholesale destruction of buildings and spaces which has usually accompanied post-war central area redevelopment aimed at accommodating the motor car. Instead, traffic management schemes, pedestrianisation, car parking charges and other measures have been used to try to keep traffic moving. It has not worked perfectly, but at least we still have the medieval city centre as well as the traffic.

Salisbury has always been an important commercial centre: it is always full of people on market days (twice a week for the last 600 years). Over the years there have been tens of thousands of little changes in the physical and social fabric of the city, even if there have been few grand, melodramatic gestures of civic pride. The camera is even better at recording these small changes, in shop fronts and signs, street furniture, people's clothes and their methods of transport and so on,

and reminds us of what has actually changed in places where we think nothing has happened.

In the countryside around Salisbury most of the villages are located in the valleys of the five rivers which join together in or just outside the city: the Avon, the Nadder, the Wylye, the Bourne and the Ebble. They include Wilton (not so much a village as a small town, one with an impressive history of its own and, in its day, a strong rival to Salisbury itself), Britford on the Avon just down stream from the city, and Coombe Bissett on the tiny river Ebble just to the south. These and many other settlements, all of historical as well as geographical interest, provide a photographic archive which perfectly complements that of the city itself, for the spire of the cathedral can be seen from most of the villages, and Francis Frith and his camera have been busy here as well. The present collection of photographs adds up to a fascinating picture of a fascinating city and is hinterland. How much of it will remain basically unaltered in another 800 years?

THE CATHEDRAL FROM THE RIVER 1887 19730

In a scene that has changed little in 100 years, the tranquil surface of the River Avon gently reflects the majesty of the Cathedral and its magnificent 404 feet spire, the highest in England. The famous water meadows on the right of the picture still exist: the fields on the left are now the Queen Elizabeth Gardens and open to the public.

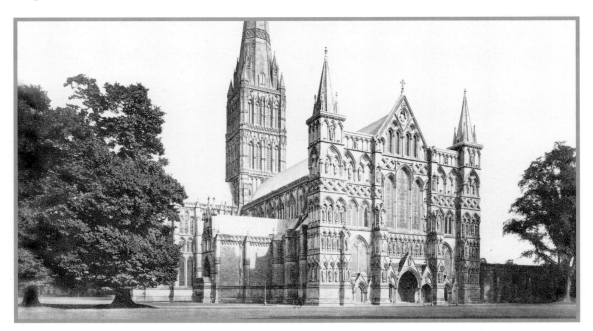

THE CATHEDRAL FROM THE NORTH-WEST c1862 1713

The imposing, dominant, west front of the cathedral is, architecturally, its least satisfying feature. It was much restored in the 19th century. The wall of the cloisters, a feature of monastic buildings, can be seen on the right of the picture, although no monks ever dwelled within these!

THE CATHEDRAL, WEST FRONT 1887 19747

Viewed from the west, the facade of the west front is dominated by the Great West Window and the Triple Arch Door. The west front of many cathedrals were intended to be showpieces. It is the only part of the cathedral to contain exterior sculptures. Currently, the frontage is undergoing restoration, intended to leave it as it originally looked in 1260AD.

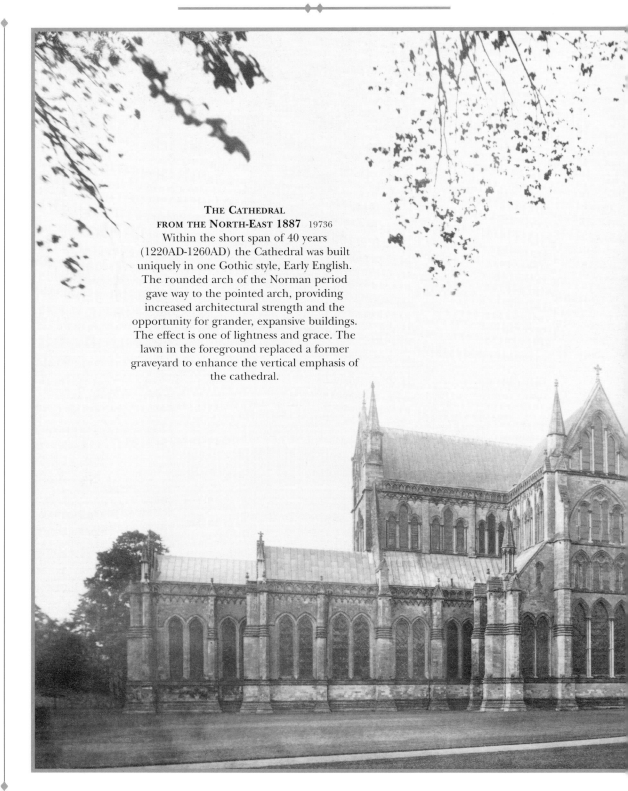

THE CATHEDRAL FROM THE NORTH-EAST 1887 19736
Within the short span of 40 years (1220AD-1260AD) the Cathedral was built uniquely in one Gothic style, Early English. The rounded arch of the Norman period gave way to the pointed arch, providing increased architectural strength and the opportunity for grander, expansive buildings. The effect is one of lightness and grace. The lawn in the foreground replaced a former graveyard to enhance the vertical emphasis of the cathedral.

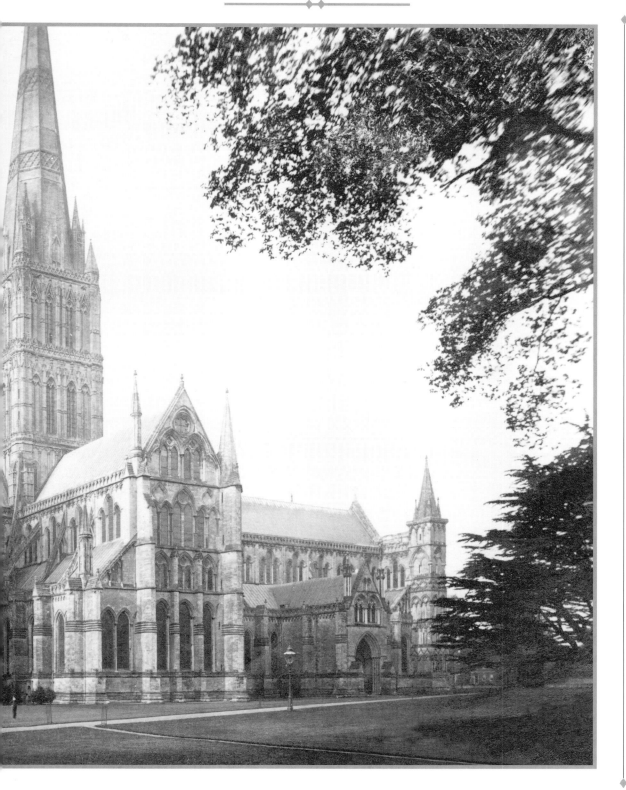

THE CATHEDRAL, CHOIR EAST 1887 19764
The interior has an impressive architectural unity. The stone is from Chilmark, ten miles to the west, and the slender black shafts supporting the arches are of Purbeck marble. The choir seats can be seen in the foreground: to the right is the canopy of the Bishop's Seat.

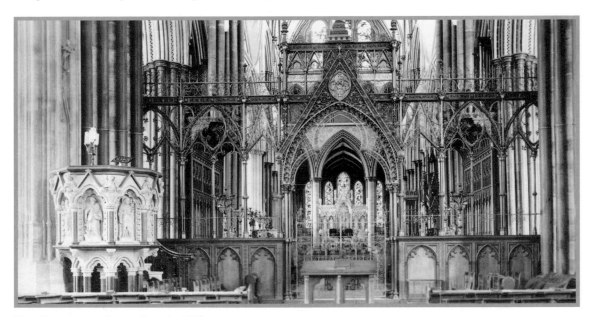

THE CATHEDRAL, CHOIR SCREEN 1887 19761
The Iron Choir Screen which separated the entrance to the choir from the nave was removed in 1959 by order of the Dean and Chapter, presumably to give an uninterrupted view from the western entrance through to the great eastern window. It was designed by Sir Giles Gilbert Scott and erected in the 19th century by Skidmore of Coventry, who specialised in ironwork.

THE CATHEDRAL FROM THE NORTH-WEST 1928

The spire was added some sixty years after the cathedral was completed in 1260AD. Block your hand over the spire and try to imagine the cathedral without it. The effect would be geometric, and your eyes would remain horizontal. In the middle ages, society and thought was stratified. The addition of the spire was intended to take your eyes upwards.

◆

HIGH STREET GATE AND THE MATRONS' COLLEGE 1906

To the right of the picture is the foliage-covered Matrons' College, built in the 1680s as a refuge for the widows of priests who were ordained in the Salisbury dioceses. It could accommodate ten matrons, who each had their own garden but had to share the water pump and the toilet. In the centre of the building is an interesting octagonal lantern with the royal coat of arms above the doorway. The plaque beneath it records the work of Bishop Seth Ward, a friend of Christopher Wren, who founded the college.

THE CATHEDRAL FROM THE NORTH-WEST 1928 80926

HIGH STREET GATE AND THE MATRONS' COLLEGE 1906 56366

HIGH STREET GATE 1894 34872

The High Street Gate (sometimes called the North Gate) is
closed every evening, a practice that has continued since a
1340AD when the wall surrounding the cathedral was
completed, thus emphasising that the cathedral and town
separate entities. It housed a night porter and a small ga

HIGH STREET GATE c1950
Looking through the gate the Crown Hotel, now no longer in existence, can be seen on the left of the High Street. Sadly, the dormer windows on the right sit uneasily with the overhanging bay window and the quaint street lantern.

◆

ST ANN'S GATE 1906
Built in 1331, St Anne's Gate links the Close with St John's Street and Exeter Street. The chapel above the gate, built into the Close wall, was used for concerts. The plaque to the right prohibits livestock and discourages motor cars from entering the Close. Note the gas street lighting and the dress of the boys in the foreground.

HIGH STREET GATE c1950 S48067

ST ANN'S GATE 1906 56367

St Ann's Gate 1911

Viewed from the Close and looking East, the room with the large window over the Gate was a chapel belonging to Malmesbury House, the front of which can be seen to the left of the picture. Malmesbury House was a 13th-century canonry, substantially rebuilt in the 17th century by Sir Christopher Wren. Charles ll stayed there; so did the composer Handel, who may well have performed there.

St Ann's Gate c1950

A later view of St Ann's Gate, with motor cars in evidence in the street scene - now, the gate can be used by pedestrians only. One of the houses on the left, known as Fielding House and now part of a school, is associated with the novelist Henry Fielding, whose wife Charlotte lived here in the 1730s.

St Ann's Gate 1911   63764

St Ann's Gate c1950   S48068

HARNHAM GATE 1906 56364

At the southern end of the Close is Harnham Gate, one of the three gates that served the cathedral; it is contemporary with the original 14th-century cathedral wall. It is the only gate without a room above it.

SOUTH CORNER OF THE CLOSE c1955 S48076

This autumn picture of Harnham Gate and the southern corner of the Close reflects then, as now, a secluded and quiet area of the Close. The house to the left of the Gate is an integral part of the wall. The house facing the photographer was built in the 18th century by John Talman, the Vicar Choral.

HARNHAM GATE c1950

The Gate leads directly to Harnham Bridge over the River Avon. This was an important medieval trading entrance to the city for traders and travellers from the west. The Close constable still locks all Gates every night. Large sections of the wall and the gateways are built from stone brought from the original cathedral at Old Sarum.

THE CLOSE 1906

This attractive view of the Close looks westwards towards Choristers Green. The original campanile (Bell Tower) was behind the house on the left of the picture, and was removed in 1789.

HARNHAM GATE c1950 S48059

THE CLOSE 1906 56371

THE CLOSE 1928 80931

THE CLOSE 1928

Two decades later the same view is as tranquil as before. The creepers have been stripped off, but little else has changed. The Doric pediment above the doorway of the house to the right reminds us of our links with classical Greece.

◆

THE CLOSE c1950

Then, as now, people visiting the cathedral have entered through the busy High Street Gate. The 1950s dress is more formal than now, and there appear to be many businessmen with briefcases. This is also a fine view of the Matrons' College with its octagonal lantern. Note also how motor cars have intruded upon the street scene.

THE CLOSE c1950 S48107

KINGS HOUSE TRAINING COLLEGE 1928
Formerly a teacher training college for schoolmistresses, since 1980 Kings House has been the Salisbury and Wiltshire museum. It was named Kings House after James I, and Queen Ann of Denmark and Henry, Prince of Wales stayed there in the early 17th century. The building is mostly 16th-century, as is shown by the wonderful stone mullions dominating its frontage; the two-storey porch on the left is even older.

◆

KINGS HOUSE TRAINING COLLEGE 1928
Another view of this fine building, as it was when it was still covered with climbing vegetation. The two-storey porch probably dates from the late 14th century.

KINGS HOUSE TRAINING COLLEGE 1928 80933

KINGS HOUSE TRAINING COLLEGE 1928 80932

POULTRY CROSS 1894 34870
Originally one of four market crosses, the Poultry Cross, at the junction of Butcher Row and Minster Street, is the only one to survive. Since 1335 it has marked the area reserved for the selling of poultry and vegetables. The cross dates from the 15th century: the upper part was restored in 1853.

POULTRY CROSS AND SILVER STREET 1906 56359
People sit and watch life go by under the hexagonal arches of the Poultry Cross. For five hundred years commerce has surrounded this area with ironmongers, shoemakers and fish and meat shops. In the background a horse-drawn cart delivers ales and beers, and K Boots and Shoes are sold at the corner shop in the background. St Thomas' church tower can be seen above and behind the roofs of the shops.

POULTRY CROSS AND SILVER STREET 1928 80918
This view of the Poultry Cross and Silver Street clearly shows a sign over Olivers' shoe shop - the only shop in this street which is still there today. The County Hotel is in the background.

POULTRY CROSS AND SILVER STREET 1928 80917
By 1928 the motor car has replaced horses. Since photograph No 56359 was taken, the shop on the corner in the middle of the picture has lost its tile-hanging, and its original timber frame has been exposed.

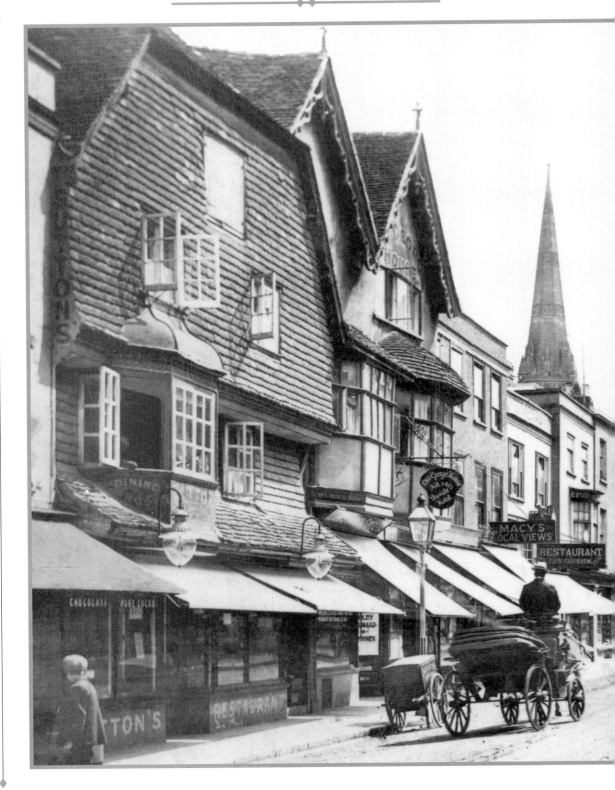

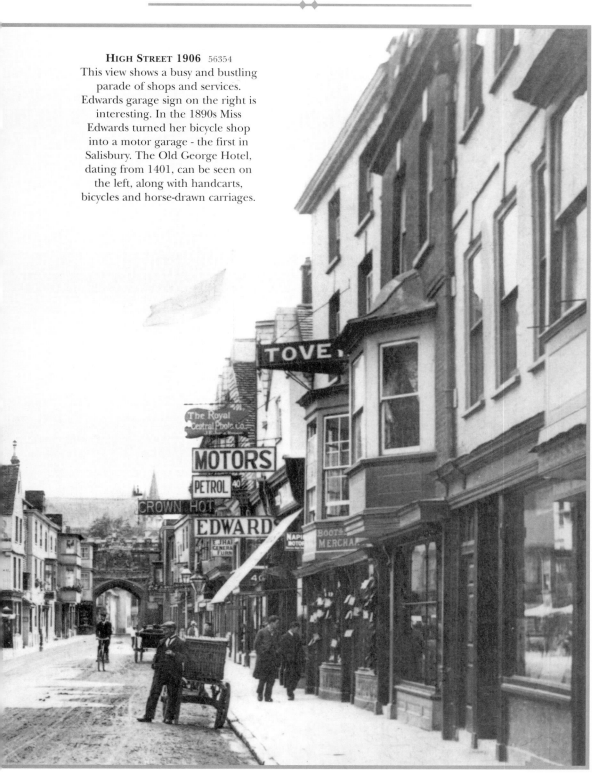

HIGH STREET 1906 56354
This view shows a busy and bustling
parade of shops and services.
Edwards garage sign on the right is
interesting. In the 1890s Miss
Edwards turned her bicycle shop
into a motor garage - the first in
Salisbury. The Old George Hotel,
dating from 1401, can be seen on
the left, along with handcarts,
bicycles and horse-drawn carriages.

HIGH STREET 1919 68969

The same view thirteen years after photograph No 56354, when the motor car and bicycle have replaced the horse and handcart. Note that everyone in the photograph is wearing a hat. Since the earlier photograph the road surface has been improved by 'metalling', and many of the old gas lamps have disappeared.

HIGH STREET 1928 80922

The store on the corner is that of W H Smith, which now occupies a different site. The perambulator in the foreground now seems decidedly old-fashioned. Driving on the left seems to have a flexible interpretation!

OLD HOUSE IN HIGH STREET 1928

This outstanding timbered-framed building was built in the 14th century and is jettied (the overhang of the first floor) on both sides. For many years it was the famous antiquarian bookshop Beach's, which survived until 1999.

NEW CANAL 1906

New Canal street commemorates one of the many open waterways which ran through the medieval streets until the 19th century. The largest of the waterways was known as Town Ditch and was filled in 1875. At the time of this photograph, the traffic is still horse-drawn and trees still grow in the street.

OLD HOUSE IN HIGH STREET 1928 80923

NEW CANAL 1906 56355

CATHERINE STREET 1906 56356
Gas street lighting was introduced in the late 19th century, and lasted until its replacement by electricity early in the 20th. The attractive lights over the shop windows would today need planning permission! In the distance the famous White Hart Hotel can be seen, with its statue above the Grecian portico on top of its huge pillars.

SILVER STREET 1906 56357

The absence of traffic allows dogs and cats to cross the road unhindered. Steven's drapery shop on the right attracts the attention of admiring customers. The Poultry Cross, referred to earlier, can just be seen on the left of the picture.

FISHERTON STREET 1906 56360

Fisherton Street was an important shopping street linking the railway station with the city centre. The church spire in the distance belongs to the Congregational church: the Angel Hotel to the left has now disappeared. The hotel porter waits hopefully outside with his hand-cart. The famous Dr Roberts' clock tower on the right of the picture was built in 1893 as a memorial to his wife. It still functions today.

FISHERTON STREET 1928 80924
'The Loves of Carmen' was showing at the Picture House in Fisherton Street when this picture was taken. Alas, like Bizet's operatic heroine, the cinema perished in the last act not long afterwards.

CHURCH HOUSE AND CRANE BRIDGE 1906 56372
The Diocesan offices are housed in this 15th-century wool merchant's house with its magnificent original oak doors. It was most likely built by William Lightfoot, mayor of Salisbury in 1451 and later MP for Salisbury. Crane Bridge carries the road over the River Avon..

THE COUNTY HOTEL AND BRIDGE STREET 1928 80925
Motorcycles with sidecars were a popular and economical means of getting about for ordinary people. The large County Hotel was built in 1874 to cater for the increase in tourism after the railway had arrived. The hotel was recently refurbished and changed its name, but its Victorian elevations remain largely unaltered. The bridge was rebuilt in 1961.

YE HALLE OF JOHN HALLE 1913 65310

In a city full of medieval gems, the Hall of John Halle stands out as an extraordinary curiosity. Behind this fake Tudor facade of the late 19th century is a house built 400 years earlier for a wool merchant who became mayor of the city. The Hall is now the entrance foyer of the Odeon Cinema which lies behind it; with its high, open timber roof and stained glass windows, it makes going to the pictures in Salisbury a unique experience. Watsons, the long-established glass and china business occupying the site in 1913, moved to Queen Street in 1931.

HIGH STREET c1955 S48135

The entrance to Barclays Bank is seen to the right of the picture. The High Street leads to the North Gate of the cathedral. It is interesting that in the right foreground a Belisha Beacon stands, before the introduction of zebra crossings. The familiar store of Boots is to the left, and W H Smith is on the corner by the car that is turning.

HIGH STREET c1955 S48122

This is a closer view of the southern end of the High Street. Street furniture is changing with the introduction of the ugly concrete street lamp post outside the timber-framed building that was Beach's bookshop. There is a striking coat of arms high up on the wall of Mitre House.

VIEW FROM THE HIGH STREET c1955 S48116

The coat of arms above the North Gate is that of James ll. Parking is beginning to present a problem. The numerous projecting first floor bay windows give period atmosphere and character to the street.

HIGH STREET GATE c1955 S48118

Looking through the Gate in to the Close, a notice on the doors is a reminder that they are shut every night at 11pm. And damage to the Gate (bottom left) is clearly the result of vehicular access.

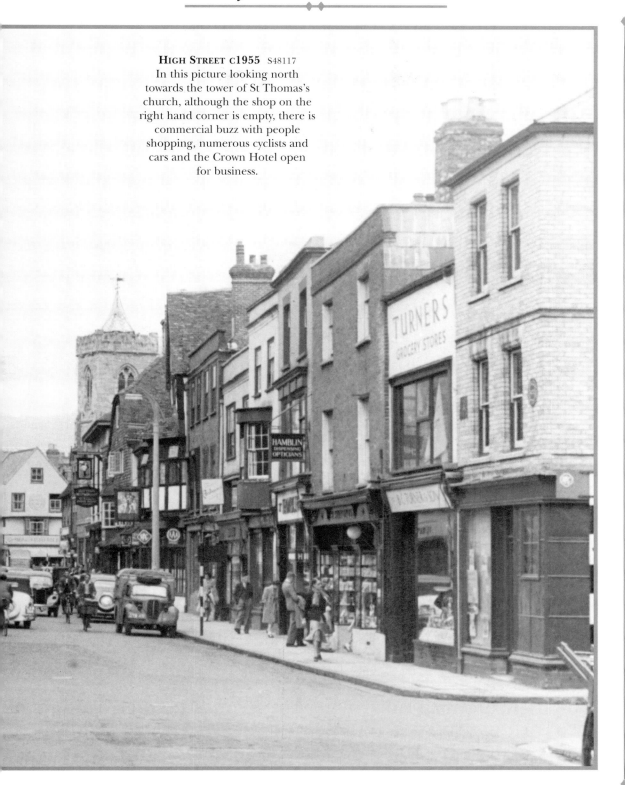

HIGH STREET c1955 S48117
In this picture looking north towards the tower of St Thomas's church, although the shop on the right hand corner is empty, there is commercial buzz with people shopping, numerous cyclists and cars and the Crown Hotel open for business.

HIGH STREET c1950 S48088

In the fifties and sixties many shops and other commercial users clearly felt they needed to advertise their presence more aggressively to passers-by. The Crown Hotel in the High Street tried very hard; but it did the proprietors no good, because the hotel closed down soon afterwards.

HIGH STREET c1955 S48140

The same view as photograph No 48117, taken some time later, shows changes. The once-empty shop is now Brittanic Assurance, and next door to Hamblins is a wallpaper shop. MacFisheries has been tile-hung, losing a top floor window, and has turned into Hepworths, the tailors. The old Crown Hotel is soon to close and become another High Street shop.

NEW STREET c1955 S48114

The right-hand side of New Street is today still largely intact, with some interesting architectural features such as red brick decorations, first floor bay windows and jettied overhangs. The left hand side of the street, in contrast, has been redeveloped as part of the Old George Mall shopping centre.

ST JOHN'S STREET c1950 S48108

St John's Street is the main entrance to the city from the south. On the left is the Close Wall and St Ann's Gate; on the right the White Hart Hotel stands out, with its giant portico surmounted by the eponymous deer. Closer to the viewer is the timber-framed King's Arms Inn, dating from the mid 17th century. It added a grand first floor dining room in the 19th century with its unusually tall pedimented window.

CATHERINE STREET c1950 S48087

This picture was probably taken soon after the end of the Second World War, judging by the Food Office sign on the right of the picture. The Bell and Crown inn is now called the Cloisters; Gibbs Mew was the main Salisbury brewery, now sadly no longer with us. The Wessex motors garage, whose signs are displayed on the facing wall, has gone, and has been replaced by an office block.

CATHERINE STREET c1955
Compared to picture No 56356 (1906),
Catherine Street looks very drab, despite
the evocatively named Cafe Rendezvous
on the left. The scene reflects the
austere post war years.

NEW CANAL c1955
Viewed from the corner of the High
Street, Boots is on the left hand side,
with W H Smith opposite. There is a
striking canopy over a former hoist at
Stokes Tea and Coffee Warehouse on the
left of the photograph.

CATHERINE STREET c1955 S48126

NEW CANAL c1955 S48113

NEW CANAL c1955 S48124
Buses, lorries, cars, bicycles and
pedestrians all jostle for position in
the widest section of New Canal.
Since World War One buses had
gradually replaced carriers
bringing people to the city,
especially on the twice-a-week
market days. This area has become
the unofficial bus station.

NEW CANAL c1950 S48091

NEW CANAL c1950
In this photograph, New Canal has become a one way street - yet it still looks congested.

◆

NEW CANAL c1950
The Wheatsheaf Public House on the right is now a jewellers shop, and Matthews, the Gillingham brewery, closed down soon after this picture was taken. The bus on the left was owned by Victory Tours of Sixpenny Handley, still a major coach company.

NEW CANAL c1950 S48105

NEW CANAL C1950 S48123

This view is looking back towards the High Street. The Southern Daily Echo (now the Southern Evening Echo) still exists, but not its Salisbury office. The famous clock above Electric House is still there. The large four-storey timber-framed building in the centre was a succession of shoe shops. Today it is the Woolwich Building Society.

MILFORD STREET AND NEW CANAL C1955 S48154

The Red Lion Hotel on the left still trades today; the facade dates from about 1820, but behind it, in the courtyard through the archway, is the original 14th-century inn. Opposite is the Cathedral Hotel, which closed a few years ago.

MILFORD STREET c1950 S48093
This view is towards Milford Hill. The Co-op is next to the Cathedral Hotel, with a shooting-brake parked outside. This is the 'new' Co-op, replacing the original which burnt down in 1937.

MILFORD STREET c1950 S48127

QUEEN STREET c1950

Clearly, it is market day on a site that has witnessed two markets a week for some 500 years. Salisbury market quickly eclipsed the older Wilton market, and was a significant factor in Salisbury's commercial success.

◆

QUEEN STREET c1950

The corner of the Guildhall building can just be seen on the left. This view looks towards Endless Street to the large vertical Bus Station sign in the distance.

QUEEN STREET c1950 S48096

QUEEN STREET c1950 S48094

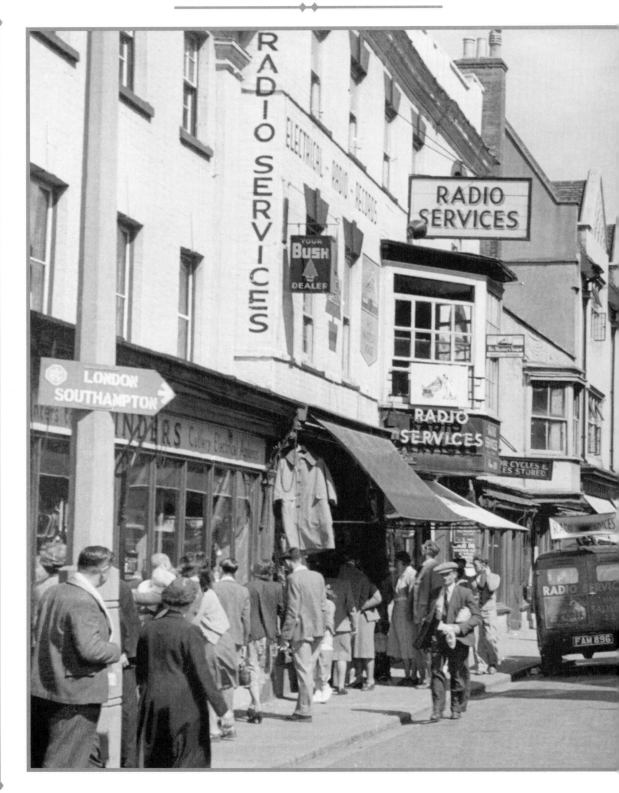

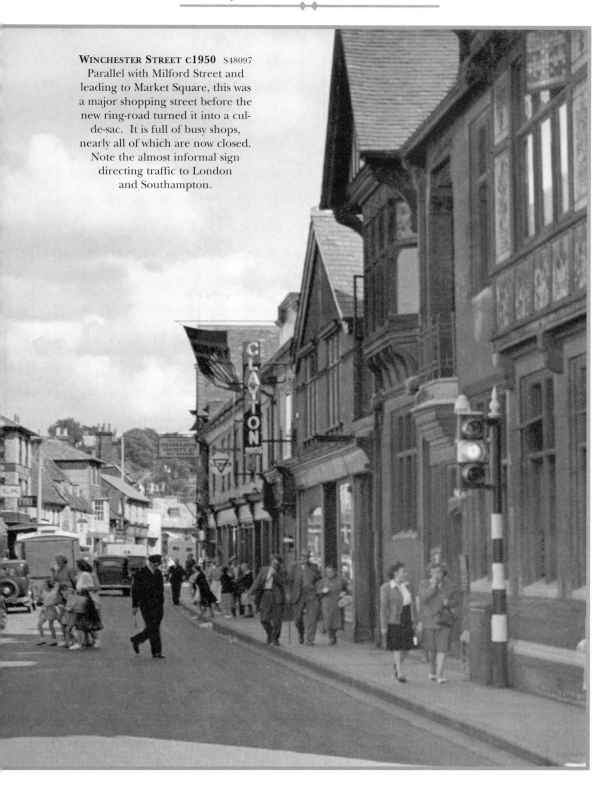

WINCHESTER STREET c1950 S48097
Parallel with Milford Street and
leading to Market Square, this was
a major shopping street before the
new ring-road turned it into a cul-
de-sac. It is full of busy shops,
nearly all of which are now closed.
Note the almost informal sign
directing traffic to London
and Southampton.

QUEEN STREET c1950 S48125

FISH ROW c1950 S48095
The importance of Salisbury to the military establishment after the war can be seen in this picture of Fish Row, just behind the Guildhall. A Pickfords lorry is fighting its way along the narrow street, possibly heading for the Military Tailors in the left foreground, or to the Servicemen's Hostel next door.

BLUE BOAR ROW c1955 S48226

This shows the main public open space in the city, the Market Square: for centuries it has been the centre of the city's business and social life, and is surrounded by many fine buildings. This view shows Blue Boar Row, looking west towards the old Cheese Market and the Market House at the end. Market House was built in 1859; it was converted to a Public Library in 1972, but the facade was kept with its three archways, iron gates and clock.

BLUE BOAR ROW c1950 S48128

In the 19th century, banks often built very imposing buildings to reflect their status in everyday life. The head office of the Wilts and Dorset Bank, built in 1869, is now Lloyds Bank, and is just one of a row of large, impressive buildings along the northern side of the Market Square.

BLUE BOAR ROW c1950 S48099

Almost the same view as photograph No S48128, but obviously taken on market day. The traders' stalls can be seen on the Market Place, and there is far more activity in the surrounding streets. The Cadena Cafe, with its resident dance band, would have been busy all day; so too would Style and Gerrish's department store (now Debenham's) next door.

POULTRY CROSS c1950 S48102

MINSTER STREET c1950 S48101

A view of one of the city's best narrow medieval streets, lined with tall, overhanging shops and houses. Almost all the buildings date from the 15th century : note the overhanging upper storeys and the timber framing. The famous Haunch of Venison Inn on the left is virtually untouched both externally and internally.

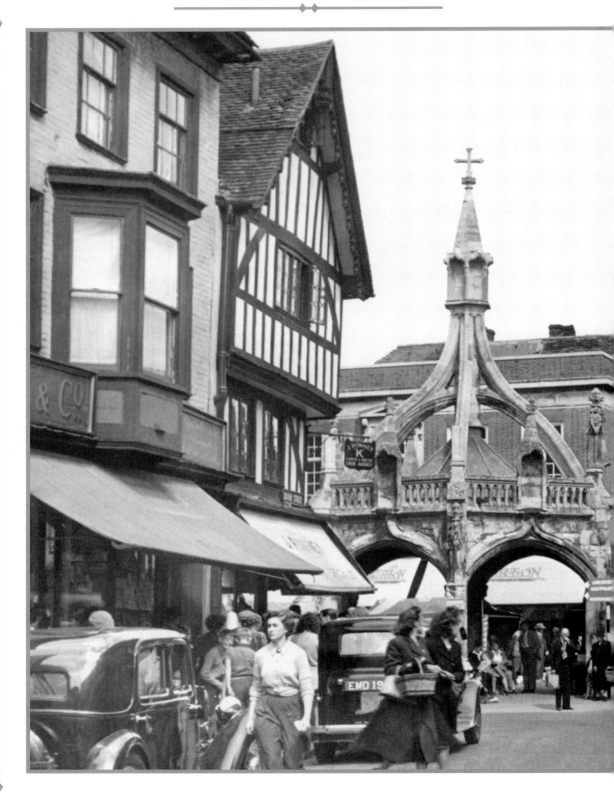

SILVER STREET c1950 S48104
This picture was probably taken on
a market day : there is so much
activity in the narrow streets
around the Poultry Cross that
conflict between vehicles and
pedestrians is inevitable.

SILVER STREET c1955 S48132

Another view of Silver Street from the corner of the High Street. Virtually every shop in the picture has since either moved elsewhere in the city centre or closed down altogether: Marks and Spencer moved to New Canal, and Woolworths to the High Street.

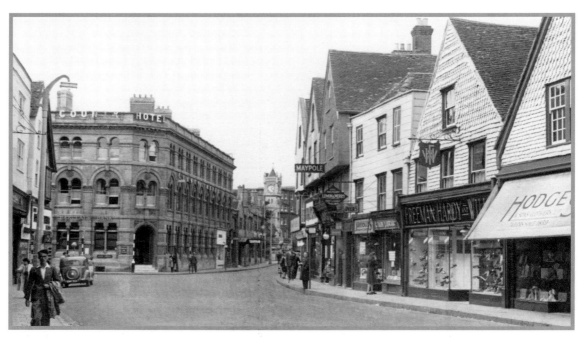

SILVER STREET AND BRIDGE STREET c1955 S48129

In this picture, the impressive County Hotel and Barclays Bank (built originally as a wine and spirit warehouse) can be seen on the corner, with the clock tower and the old Infirmary beyond.

BRIDGE STREET c1955

This picture gives a closer view of the fine Victorian architecture in Bridge Street. The Clock Tower, across the bridge, was built by a Doctor Roberts in 1893 on the site of the old County Gaol. The much older Infirmary beyond has since been converted to flats.

FISHERTON STREET c1955

Like many other shopping streets in Salisbury, Fisherton Street has changed very little over the last fifty years, in spite of most of the shops themselves moving or closing down and being replaced by new ones. Asbridge the Optician is one that remains to this day, although its unusual hanging sign (on the extreme left of the picture) has long since disappeared.

BRIDGE STREET c1955 S48134

FISHERTON STREET c1955 S48145

THE GODOLPHIN SCHOOL 1928 80934

The school was founded in 1726 as an endowed charity school for 'orphan gentlewomen borne of parents of the Church of England'. For many years it occupied various premises in the Close, including Kings House, before moving from the damp, riverside site in 1847, apparently to escape a cholera epidemic. Its more salubrious site was, and remains, the one pictured here on Milford Hill, just east of the city centre beyond the ring road.

RIVER WALK 1923 74229

This view shows the walk alongside what is now Churchill Gardens to south of the city. The bridge in the distance is the old Harnham or Ayleswade Bridge and the view was taken before the building of New Bridge Road in 1931.

FISHERTON MILL FROM LONGBRIDGE c1955

This was a large mill on the River Nadder just upstream from the confluence with the Avon. The Millers House seen here is all that remains of a much larger building; it is now almost invisible from the bridge downstream because the trees and riverside vegetation have grown so much.

OLD SARUM, FROM THE SOUTH 1913

This picture is taken from the area of Hudson's field, looking northwards to the hill of Old Sarum. Castle Road (part of the A345) is on the right, and the Avon Valley is just out of the picture to the left. The scene has not changed too much today, as the suburban growth of New Sarum has stopped short of the site of its neolithic ancestor.

FISHERTON MILL FROM LONGBRIDGE c1955 S48052

OLD SARUM, FROM THE SOUTH 1913 65294

OLD SARUM, THE CASTLE, INTERIOR OF POSTERN TOWER 1913

Old Sarum was originally an Iron Age fort with earth ramparts. The Normans fortified the existing site using local and occasionally unstable building materials. This picture shows the remains of the flint tower, which, as can be seen, needed substantial reinforcement with solid blocks of stone.

OLD SARUM, THE GARDEROBE PITS AND THE FOUNDATION OF THE GREAT TOWER 1913

The garderobe pits - the medieval toilets - are shown on the foreground, with the stone and flint walls of the tower behind. Flint walls were normally supported on firm stone foundations owing to their brittle and uneven structure.

OLD SARUM, THE CASTLE, INTERIOR OF POSTERN TOWER 1913
65296

OLD SARUM, THE GARDEROBE PITS AND THE FOUNDATION OF THE GREAT TOWER 1913 65300

OLD SARUM, OBJECTS DISCOVERED DURING EXCAVATIONS 1913 65303

Old Sarum, an Iron Age fort, a junction for four Roman roads, a cathedral town and the original Salisbury, reveals its past with this display of excavated artefacts. Medieval jugs, iron keys, Norman stonework and animal bones bring together its troubled and relatively short-lived past.

WILTON, WILTON HOUSE, FRONT ENTRANCE 1919 68931

This is the forecourt at the north front of Wilton House. The house was built for the first Earl of Pembroke when he was granted the old nunnery estate after its dissolution in 1544. His descendants have lived here ever since.

WILTON, WEST STREET 1919 68944
This picture looks westwards from the market place in the centre of Wilton. The bell tower of the Italianate church of St Mary and St Nicholas is clearly visible along West Street.

WILTON, THE SQUARE 1919 68943

Wilton, once the capital of Wessex, was the most important town in early medieval Wiltshire. This is Kingsbury Square, with St Edith's church on the left. The road across the square is the A30.

WILTON, THE SQUARE c1965 W166066

In this view of the Market Place, the vehicles in the car park are typical of the period, and the van in the centre probably came from RAF Chilmark nearby. Since then most of the shops in the picture - and the RAF base - have gone.

COOMBE BISSETT, THE VILLAGE c1955 C299005
The stone bridge carries the A354 over the River Ebble at Coombe Bisset. It was built in about 1780, at a time when the new turnpike roads were contributing significantly to Salisbury's commercial development, and it is pictured here viewed from the original packhorse bridge, just downstream, which it replaced.

COOMBE BISSETT, THE VILLAGE c1955 C299001
This picture shows the River Ebble and the A354 Blandford Road running side-by-side through the village of Coombe Bissett, a couple of miles south of Salisbury. The barn on the left has now been converted into a house.

COOMBE BISSETT, THE VILLAGE c1955 C299003
In this view the pub, the river, and both bridges can all be seen. Note the pole sign for the pub standing in the river.

COOMBE BISSETT
The Church c1955
St Michael's church in Coombe Bisset is a mixture of architectural styles. It has a picturesque traditional setting: a farmyard, a graveyard, a war memorial and a yew tree.

COOMBE BISSETT, THE CHURCH c1955 C299008

COOMBE BISSETT, THE VILLAGE c1955 C299006

BRITFORD, THE CHURCH 1906 56382

Britford is a tiny village just outside Salisbury to the south east. It is situated on the Avon in an extensive and complex area of water meadows and carriers which control the flow of the river downstream. The parish church is extremely old and surprisingly large, with parts dating from Norman and even Saxon times.

BRITFORD, MOAT HOUSE 1906 56381

The Moat, or Moat House, is a splendid large manor house begun in Georgian times and surrounded, as the name suggests, by water.

BRITFORD, THE VILLAGE 1906 56380
Maybe the unmetalled roads in all villages looked like this after a heavy storm in 1906, but this scene is also a reminder of Britford's close proximity to the Avon.

SALISBURY, FROM HARNHAM 1906 56353
The Cathedral spire dominated the surrounding countryside in previous centuries just as it does today. This view is from Harnham Hill, looking north eastwards across the Avon and an area of farmland which is just beginning to become built-up as the suburb of Harnham. In the middle distance, to the left of the Cathedral, is the old Infirmary and the Congregational church; on the right, closer to the camera, is the Church of All Saints in Harnham.

HARNHAM, THE VILLAGE 1906 56377
This picture is taken at the top of old
Harnham Road, looking back down
towards the bridge. The cottages on
the right are still there today, but
much else has changed - and not
many people would sit with their
children at the side of the road!

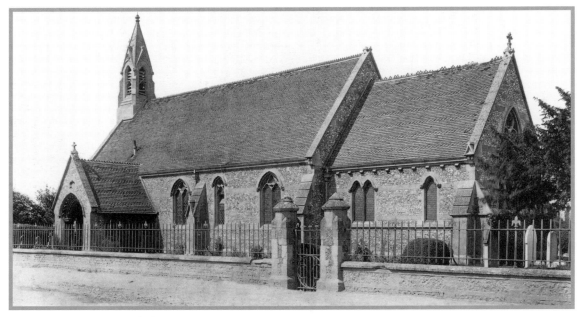

HARNHAM, THE CHURCH 1906 56379

The Victorian Church of All Saints in Harnham was built in 1854 and dedicated to the memory of a former Dean of Salisbury Cathedral. Today, heavy traffic thunders close by on the road in the foreground (the A3094), but drivers do not see the church because of the screen of trees which has grown up along the wall in front of it.

SALISBURY, HARNHAM BRIDGE 1928 80937

The bridge was built by the Bishop of Salisbury around 1240 to facilitate trade between the new city and the south: the Cathedral spire can be seen in the background. Nearly seven hundred years later, the bridge was still carrying all south-bound traffic around the city and across the Avon, but a new bridge was built just downstream in 1931.

SALISBURY
De Vaux Place 1928

On the Salisbury side of Harnham Bridge, De Vaux Place leads to The Close - the Harnham Gate is at the far end of the wall. Most of the old houses here were built in the 18th and 19th centuries using stone from the remains of the De Vaux College, which was established here by the Bishop to train the clergy as early as 1262 - probably the first university college in the century.

◆

SALISBURY
The Cathedral from Old Mill, Harnham c1955

The Cathedral viewed from the south has been a favourite subject for artists - including, of course, Constable. This particular view is from the Old Mill at Harnham, and shows the Mill itself, the river and the water meadows as well as the Cathedral. Harnham Mill is a very old building, dating from around 1500, which has had a number of different uses (it is currently a restaurant and guest house). Note the flint-and-ashlar chequered walling - the best example of this technique in the area. Like the first photograph in this book, the timeless beauty of this scene has remained unchanged for more than half a millennium.

SALISBURY, DE VAUX PLACE 1928 80930

SALISBURY, THE CATHEDRAL FROM OLD MILL, HARNHAM c1955 S48056

Index

Frith Book Co 1999 Titles

From 2000 we aim at publishing 100 new books each year. For latest catalogue please contact Frith Book Co

Barnstaple	1-85937-084-5	£12.99	Oct 99		Maidstone	1-85937-056-X	£12.99	Sep 99
Blackpool	1-85937-049-7	£12.99	Sep 99		Northumberland & Tyne and Wear	1-85937-072-1	£14.99	Sep 99
Bognor Regis	1-85937-055-1	£12.99	Sep 99		North Yorkshire	1-85937-048-9	£14.99	Sep 99
Bristol	1-85937-050-0	£12.99	Sep 99		Nottingham	1-85937-060-8	£12.99	Sep 99
Cambridge	1-85937-092-6	£12.99	Oct 99		Oxfordshire	1-85937-076-4	£14.99	Oct 99
Cambridgeshire	1-85937-086-1	£14.99	Nov 99		Penzance	1-85937-069-1	£12.99	Sep 99
Cheshire	1-85937-045-4	£14.99	Sep 99		Reading	1-85937-087-X	£12.99	Nov 99
Chester	1-85937-090-X	£12.99	Nov 99		St Ives	1-85937-068-3	£12.99	Sep 99
Chesterfield	1-85937-071-3	£12.99	Sep 99		Salisbury	1-85937-091-8	£12.99	Nov 99
Chichester	1-85937-089-6	£12.99	Nov 99		Scarborough	1-85937-104-3	£12.99	Sep 99
Cornwall	1-85937-054-3	£14.99	Sep 99		Scottish Castles	1-85937-077-2	£14.99	Oct 99
Cotswolds	1-85937-099-3	£14.99	Nov 99		Sevenoaks and Tonbridge	1-85937-057-8	£12.99	Sep 99
					Sheffield and S Yorkshire	1-85937-070-5	£12.99	Sep 99
					Shropshire	1-85937-083-7	£14.99	Nov 99
					Southampton	1-85937-088-8	£12.99	Nov 99
					Staffordshire	1-85937-047-0	£14.99	Sep 99
					Stratford upon Avon	1-85937-098-5	£12.99	Nov 99
					Suffolk	1-85937-074-8	£14.99	Oct 99
					Surrey	1-85937-081-0	£14.99	Oct 99
					Torbay	1-85937-063-2	£12.99	Sep 99
					Wiltshire	1-85937-053-5	£14.99	Sep 99

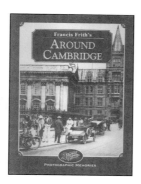

Derby	1-85937-046-2	£12.99	Sep 99
Devon	1-85937-052-7	£14.99	Sep 99
Dorset	1-85937-075-6	£14.99	Oct 99
Dorset Coast	1-85937-062-4	£14.99	Sep 99
Dublin	1-85937-058-6	£12.99	Sep 99
East Anglia	1-85937-059-4	£14.99	Sep 99
Eastbourne	1-85937-061-6	£12.99	Sep 99
English Castles	1-85937-078-0	£14.99	Oct 99
Essex	1-85937-082-9	£14.99	Nov 99
Falmouth	1-85937-066-7	£12.99	Sep 99
Hampshire	1-85937-064-0	£14.99	Sep 99
Hertfordshire	1-85937-079-9	£14.99	Nov 99
Isle of Man	1-85937-065-9	£14.99	Sep 99
Liverpool	1-85937-051-9	£12.99	Sep 99

British Life A Century Ago

246 x 189mm 144pp, hardback. Black and white Lavishly illustrated with photos from the turn of the century, and with extensive commentary. It offers a unique insight into the social history and heritage of bygone Britain.

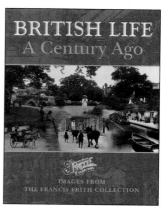

1-85937-103-5 £17.99

Available from your local bookshop or from the publisher

FRITH PRODUCTS & SERVICES

Francis Frith would doubtless be pleased to know that the pioneering publishing venture he started in 1860 still continues today. More than a hundred and thirty years later, The Francis Frith Collection continues in the same innovative tradition and is now one of the foremost publishers of vintage photographs in the world. Some of the current activities include:

Interior Decoration

Today Frith's photographs can be seen framed and as giant wall murals in thousands of pubs, restaurants, hotels, banks, retail stores and other public buildings throughout the country. In every case they enhance the unique local atmosphere of the places they depict and provide reminders of gentler days in an increasingly busy and frenetic world.

Product Promotions

Frith products have been used by many major companies to promote the sales of their own products or to reinforce their own history and heritage. Brands include Hovis bread, Courage beers, Scots Porage Oats, Colman's mustard, Cadbury's foods, Mellow Birds coffee, Dunhill pipe tobacco, Guinness, and Bulmer's Cider.

Genealogy and Family History

As the interest in family history and roots grows world-wide, more and more people are turning to Frith's photographs of Great Britain for images of the towns, villages and streets where their ancestors lived; and, of course, photographs of the churches and chapels where their ancestors were christened, married and buried are an essential part of every genealogy tree and family album.

A series of easy-to-use CD Roms is planned for publication, and an increasing number of Frith photographs will be able to be viewed on specialist genealogy sites. A growing range of Frith books will be available on CD.

The Internet

Already thousands of Frith photographs can be viewed and purchased on the internet. By the end of the year 2000 some 60,000 Frith photographs will be available on the internet. The number of sites is constantly expanding, each focussing on different products and services from the Collection.

Some of the sites are listed below.

www.townpages.co.uk
www.familystorehouse.com
www.britannia.com
www.icollector.com
www.barclaysquare.co.uk
www.cornwall-online.co.uk

For background information on the Collection look at the two following sites:

www.francisfrith.com
www.francisfrith.co.uk

Frith Products

All Frith photographs are available Framed or just as Mounted Prints, and can be ordered from the address below. From time to time other products - Address Books, Calendars, Table Mats, Postcards etc - are available.

The Frith Collectors' Guild

In response to the many customers who enjoy collecting Frith photographs we have created the Frith Collectors' Guild. Members are entitled to a range of benefits, including a regular magazine, special discounts and special limited edition products.

For further information: if you would like further information on any of the above aspects of the Frith business please contact us at the address below:

The Francis Frith Collection, Frith's Barn, Teffont, Salisbury, Wiltshire England SP3 5QP.
Tel: +44 (0) 1722 716 376 Fax: +44 (0) 1722 716 881   Email: frithbook.co.uk

To receive your FREE Mounted Print

Cut out this Voucher and return it with your remittance for £1.50 to cover postage and handling. Choose any photograph included in this book. Your SEPIA print will be A4 in size, and mounted in a cream mount with burgundy rule lines, overall size 14 x 11 inches.

Order additional Mounted Prints at HALF PRICE (only £7.49 each*)

If there are further pictures you would like to order, possibly as gifts for friends and family, acquire them at half price (no additional postage and handling required).

Have your Mounted Prints framed*

For an additional £14.95 per print you can have your chosen Mounted Print framed in an elegant polished wood and gilt moulding, overall size 16 x 13 inches (no additional postage and handling required).

---

* IMPORTANT!
These special prices are only available if ordered using the original voucher on this page (no copies permitted) and at the same time as your free Mounted Print, for delivery to the same address

---

Voucher for FREE and Reduced Price Frith Prints

Picture no.	Page number	Qty	Mounted @ £7.49	Framed + £14.95	Total Cost
		1	Free of charge*	£	£
			£	£	£
			£	£	£
			£	£	£
			£	£	£
			£	£	£

Title: SALISBURY

091-8

* Post & handling	£1.50
Total Order Cost	£

Please do not photocopy this voucher. Only the original is valid, so please cut it out and return it to us.

I enclose a cheque / postal order for £. . . . .
made payable to 'The Francis Frith Collection'
OR please debit my Mastercard / Visa / Switch / Amex card

Number . . . .

Expires . . . .   Signature . . . .

Name Mr/Mrs/Ms . . . .

Address . . . .

. . . .

. . . .

. . . .

. . . . Postcode . . . .

Daytime Tel No . . . .   Valid to 31/12/01

Frith Collectors' Guild

From time to time we publish a magazine of news and stories about Frith photographs and further special offers of Frith products. If you would like 12 months FREE membership, please return this form and we will send you a New Member Pack.

Send completed forms to:
The Francis Frith Collection, Frith's Barn, Teffont, Salisbury, Wiltshire SP3 5QP

The Francis Frith Collectors' Guild

I would like to receive the New Members Pack offering 12 months FREE membership.

091-8

Name Mr/Mrs/Ms . . . .

Address . . . .

. . . .

. . . .

. . . . Postcode . . . .

Free Print - see overleaf